MW00933515

Michael Luck

VOODOO

For Beginners

A COMPLETE GUIDE TO DISCOVER THE SECRETS OF VOODOO SPELLS, HAITIAN VODOU, AND NEW ORLEANS VOODOO RITUALS

Copyright © 2021 publishing.

All rights reserved.

Author: Michael Luck

No part of this publication may be reproduced, distributed or transmitted in any form or by any means, including photocopying recording or other electronic or mechanical methods or by any information storage and retrieval system without the prior written permission of the publisher, except in the case of brief quotation embodies in critical reviews and certain other non-commercial uses permitted by copyright law.

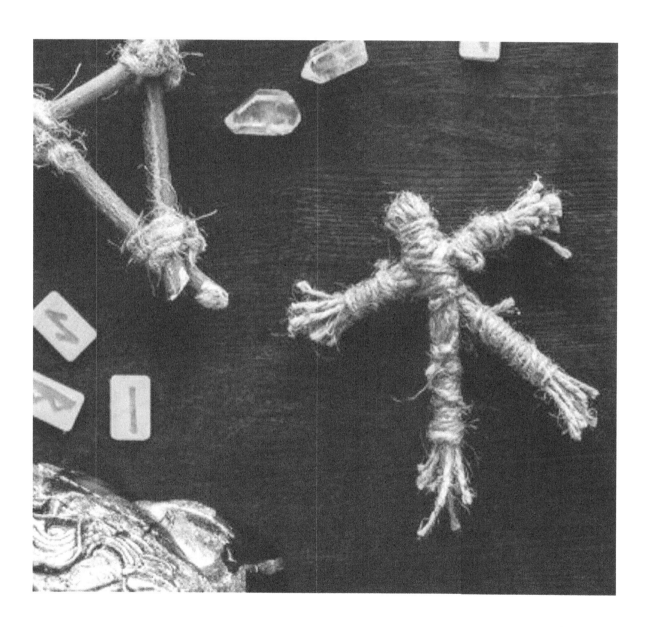

Table of Contents

Introduction...5

Chapter One. Understanding Voodoo...................................... 10

Chapter Two. Element of Voodoo 16

Chapter Three. Building Your Voodoo Shrine 27

Chapter Four. The Voodoo Doll.. 42

Chapter Five. Voodoo Queens, Kings, and Loa........................57

Chapter Six.   Invocation and Summoning Ritual 76

Chapter Seven. Health Rituals... 94

Chapter Eight. Spiritual Cleansing 107

Conclusion 123

Introduction

Voodoo isn't just any old superstition; it's an ancient form of mystical spirituality that originated in Africa and found its way into the Americas through Louisiana and New Orleans. It draws on both Christian traditions and West African faiths, blending them seamlessly without either side dominating the other.

Voodoo describes the religion that crept into New Orleans after the discovery of the Louisiana colony. It combined syncretistic Christian beliefs with traditional African and pre-Christian religions. The Catholic Church viewed it as a threat to Christianity, but it was too entrenched in too many communities to be expelled entirely. So it coexisted with Catholicism while retaining many of its traditions and practices.

Along with the African religions brought to the New World, Voodoo developed as an adaptation of many Native American spiritual beliefs and practices. Some of these rituals have been carried on through modern-day practitioners and are expressed in traditional hoodoo, a seemingly harmless form of magic. It's not harmless at all.

The Voodoo religion is an eclectic combination of Roman Catholic religions, West African religions, and traditional practices. The word "Voodoo" originates from the Fon language of Dahomey and means "spirit" or "demon." Explanations for why some people practice the religion include that a demon is using them in Possession of magic powers or that the deity is tricking them into doing bad things for a good reason.

Voodoo has many different names. In German-speaking countries, it is called Vodun. In Afrikaans, Voodoo is called Vodou, and in French, it is referred to as Vaudou. In the United States, the term "VooDoo" or "Voodoo" was used when practicing the religion. It was also called "Vaudoux", especially in Louisiana, where a large population of people practiced it in secret.

In order to understand Voodoo, one must begin with its roots in West Africa. The individual who is credited with bringing religion to the New World is a man named Houngan Zaka. He was a prince who converted to Roman Catholic Christianity and then began preaching the religion in the countryside. He was eventually captured and burned at stake, but Voodoo continued to spread throughout West Africa despite this. The slaves who were brought to Haiti and other areas of the New World practiced Voodoo as their version of Catholicism, which made it easy for them to blend in with their neighbors.

After the Caribbean slave trade was abolished, people continued to practice their version of Voodoo in secret. In 1906 a priest named François Laval Zeno reopened the first Church of Voodoo in the city of Port-au-Prince, Haiti. To differentiate between Catholicism and Voodiew, many would refer to their religion as "Vodou" or "Voodoo," depending on which country they had come from. Today there are hundreds of churches across Haiti that practice this religion.

In developing their own religion, the slaves would use Catholic icons from their masters and then remove the Christian influence by painting them black or red. The slaves also created a mythological figure known as Baron Samedi. There are also many similarities in the iconography of Voodoo and Catholicism; clearly, African influence can be seen with crosses, bibles, torches, candles, bells, and crowns.

The symbol most commonly associated with Voodoo is the cross. In many countries where Voodoo is practiced, it is considered a public offense to carve and carve the cross into a tree. In Haiti, there are many crosses carved into trees in people's yards for this purpose. The cross is also used to represent Christ and his crucifixion, while the dove represents the Holy Spirit. Many other symbols can be found in Voodoo imagery; voodoo dolls and pins, for example, are often typical of this religion. Voodoo was also initially a semi-secret religion, so many symbols, such as the cross, were difficult to understand.

The Voodoo religion is known for its use of charms. Many of these charms are intended to help people and protect them from harm or evil spirits. Voodoo practitioners can purchase these charms in many different locations, including voodoo shops and stores, secret societies, and occult clubs.

Voodoo practitioners also use many different items in their practice of religion. One such item is the voodoo doll. This doll is typically made of wax and then dressed in clothing that reflects a person's problem. The doll may then be pierced with pins or nails that reflect the particular problems of the practitioner, or they may be tied up with string to symbolize problems with physical pain or illness. These dolls are also used as part of a ceremony to keep away evil spirits or harm them if necessary.

Voodoo practitioners often use a ritual known as "Rencontre de la mort," or meeting with death. This ritual is based on the concept that an evil spirit will die if all of the offerings placed on an altar are removed.

Voodoo iconography, such as this altar, is abundant in New Orleans and other cities where large Voodoo-practicing communities exist

Two other important practices in Voodoo are "dahouen" (prayer) and "houngan" (priest). The word "houngan" has a Fon origin and refers to an African priest. There are many different houngans, many of whom are women. Many houngans can be considered chiefs of their community. Dahouen is a term used in Haiti to define types of prayers that have healing powers or help the practitioner perform acts that will harm this life or the next.

Chapter One. Understanding Voodoo

History

Voodoo is a practice that originated in Africa and was carried to the Caribbean, where it became known as Vodou. It has been practiced for centuries - some say longer than both Christianity and Islam (though nobody seems to know this for sure).

The word "voodoo" derives from the Fon language of West Africa, where "vo" means spirit or soul – so people who believe in voodoo believe that they can create a personal relationship with their ancestors through ritual worship.

The voodoo practice originated from Western African countries, commonly referred to as the Kongo and the Yoruba. This practice was brought to the Caribbean by slaves who were taken to work on plantations during the 17th and 18th centuries. In Haiti, a country in the Caribbean, still many people still worship ancestors or law. Many believe that this is how voodoo came to be practiced in Haiti.

The word "vaudou" is the Haitian Creole version of voodoo. The practice has been called "Vodou" by people who are from Haiti and other Caribbean islands. However, in the United States, many people refer to it as voodoo, and it has even been called houngan (Haitian Creole) or swi (Jamaican).

Parallels may be drawn between the religion and the practices of Haitian Voudou and other similar African-based religions, such as Yoruba. Many other American indigenous religions also share features of Voudoun. In particular, divination, ritual drumming, spirit possession trance states, etc., are common characteristics among many Native American religions.

Vodou was brought to the United States primarily through enslaved people from Haiti as well as West African slaves who were working on sugar plantations in the southern states. Roughly half of the Southern plantation owners were French while a third of them were Scots-Irish; many others were from England, Germany, and elsewhere. Prayers, various spells, charms, and fetishes left over from European practices were combined with the African origins to create what we now know of as Vodou today.

Because of the widespread practice of Vodou in Haiti, many people fled there after the slave trade ended.

In New Orleans, due to its large population of people with ties to Haiti, Voodoo has had a long history within the city. In 1804, the legislature outlawed practices labeled as "Negro magic," including Vodou. African slaves were forced to abandon their traditional religions and were assigned Catholic saints instead. From 1803-1804, the Louisiana Legislature took steps to outlaw Vodou and took even stronger steps from 1814–1819.

In spite of the efforts of both Catholic and Protestant churches to eradicate it, a strong Vodou tradition developed in New Orleans. In 1817, Louisiana became the first place in the United States to have a legal slave market. The peak period of African importation was during this period (between 1830 and 1860). Many coastal cities around the nation had similar markets.

The final chapter of this legislation came in 1877 when the legislature abolished slavery. Vodou continued to be practiced and has remained an integral part of the city.

It is still practiced today, as a large percentage of the population is descended from African slaves who came from Haiti during that period and their descendants. In addition, there are small numbers of Middle Eastern Arabs and Italian immigrants who also maintain Voodoo practices. The number of followers has been declining in recent years, however.

In New Orleans, it is most commonly practiced in the Quarter and the Garden District.

In contemporary mainstream American culture, Voodoo is viewed negatively. This stereotype has persisted even though most people who practice Voodoo do not believe in Satan. Voodoo has become associated with darker elements of the religion, such as animal sacrifice, snake handling, black magic, etc. However, this is still usually practiced within a religious context rather than a ceremonial one.

Essentials

Voodoo is the practice of sorcery that originated in the Caribbean and was spread to New Orleans by slaves, where it became an integral part of African American folk magic. It has since spread worldwide with a wide variety of practitioners, including some self-proclaimed "Goddess worshippers." Voodoo is not just a religion; it's a way of life. One popular view sees voodoo as a form of prayer, while others see it as magical or spiritual warfare that can help you achieve certain goals and success in your life.

In one view of voodoo, the term is used to refer to vodun , a spiritualist religion focused on ancestral worship, spirit possession, and animism practiced by the West African diaspora in the Americas, which can be seen as originating from a spirit cult. Second usage is in reference to traditional African religions, also called "African Traditional Religion", with practitioners calling themselves "voduns" (singular named vodun). A third form uses the term "voodoo" for any kind of magic or sorcery.

A voodoo doll is intended to represent a person, the life force (soul) of which can be manipulated in various ways, even destroyed; all this is believed to result in real-life effects on the corresponding person. Voodoo dolls are also used for healing and can be utilized in different ways. Some people may caress it or use it as an aid for visualization during meditation. After its construction, it should be given a good smell of patchouli oil before you wrap it with a red cloth. Some people wear it on themselves and leave it for a calling ritual. The voodoo doll is also used to make charms for protection, and it can also be used in banishing rituals.

Chapter Two. Element of Voodoo

Voodoo has proven itself to be an adaptable, growing, and evolving religion throughout the years - a testament, perhaps, to the resilience of the Africans who were sold in slavery and who kept its practice alive throughout their servitude. But Voodoo is perhaps also one of the most misunderstood religions globally - mainly because what little we know of it is based on what we have seen in films or read about in books. But all of it is fiction, and their sole purpose is to entertain.

But while none of these fictional accounts presume to teach factual history, the impression it has made on the public mind certainly has been remarkable. Perhaps because Voodoo rituals are so rich in color, so different in context, language, and worldview from the main world religions, people cannot help but be impressed by these selected presentations of only small portions of this religion. These days, the word Voodoo raises images of zombies and dolls with pins sticking out of them - but this is only what media has conditioned our minds to assume when we hear the word voodoo automatically.

In this chapter, we take a closer look at some of the essential elements of the practice of Voodoo, its cosmology, and how it affects and influences the lifestyle and worldview of its practitioners.

Belief in a Divine Creator

Even before the arrival of the major religions of Christianity and Islam, the Voudons believed in a supreme being or a divine creator, which they call Mahou, or Mawu. This is a transcendent Supreme Being, the creator of the universe and the world.

But this divine being does not figure prominently in people's lives. Probably because of his very transcendence, a person can only form a relationship with this divine being, in fact, through the intercession of spirits. Many of the practices of Voodoo faithful are thus centered around their relationship with spirits or the Vodun.

The god Mawu is omnipotent but essentially aloof from the concerns of man. He is both unknowable and remote from worldly affairs. But Mawu delegated his powers to the Voduns or the spirits. In essence, the Voduns are Mawu's representatives on earth, and all acts of the Voduns are essentially attributable to Mawu. But his very transcendence keeps him inexplicable and incomprehensible to people. So one cannot really find any direct worship of this divine being in Voodoo practices, save from scattered and vague references such as "God will act" or "God decides."

Vodoo Spirits, Animism, and Ancestor Worship

Voodoo practitioners believe in a Divine Creator, but this god is a distant figure that one can only communicate with through the spirits. So spirits and spirit communication is more prominent in Voodoo practice over an all-powerful deity. The term voodoo, in fact, literally means "spirit" in the local Fon language of modern-day Benin.

Voodoo practitioners believe in the power of spirits, which influence nature and human existence. Each of the many spirits is responsible for the various domains or facets of life. There are thousands of spirits called "Loa" or "Iwa," some of which are the souls of the deceased. These spirits can also act as intermediaries between the living and God. This central belief in the power of spirits seems to be a unique combination of animism and ancestor worship. The spirits of dead ancestors and the spirits of natural elements are powerful forces to which a person can turn for help.

Many of the actual practices of the Voodoo faithful are centered around their relationship with spirits. And contact with spirits is direct - the most direct of which, perhaps, is spirit possession.

When a person becomes possessed by a spirit, he becomes the god himself. The spirits incarnate in the person's body, thus enabling the spirit to walk among the living literally.

This is perhaps what gave rise to the concept of zombies - or the dead walking among the living. This is believed to take place during ritualistic dances which revere the spirit of their ancestors - and the power of the dead who are once again brought to life are so great that it is believed that touching one who is possessed of a spirit will be enough to kill you.

Some Voduns were once living - the spirits of dead ancestors who are often considered clan protectors. Ancestors who have passed on are believed to exist as spirits capable of interceding in human affairs. This particular element of Voodoo has always been present, but it is possible that it grew more prominent when the African slaves found themselves in conditions of forced servitude in a new land, strange surroundings, and were then expected to adopt a foreign religion. As they sought the familiarity of their own traditional beliefs, they also turned to the spirits of their ancestors for help in surviving what must have been a very painful transition.

Other spirits are considered the "sons of Mawu," of which there is a great number. But we can identify at least seven of those which are considered most important:

- **Sakpata** - the eldest son, and the Vodun of the earth, illness and healing, and to whom the earth was entrusted, represented by black, white, and red spots, as well as scissors

- **Xêvioso** *(or* **Xêbioso)** - the Vodun of the sky, and also of justice, and is represented by a thunderbolt, the ram, fire, and the double ax

- **Agbe** - the Vodun of the sea, and is represented by a serpent, considered a symbol of life

- **Gu** - the Vodun of iron and war, and metes out justice even to accomplices of those guilty of acts of infamy

- **Agê** - the Vodun of agriculture, forests, animals, and birds

- **Jo** - the Vodun of air and invisibility

- **Lêgba -** the youngest son and a Vodun who received no gifts because these had already been spread out among his elder brothers. He is therefore jealous, a wild card among the pantheon, thus he is considered Vodun of the unpredictable, of all else that cannot be assigned to the others, of daily tragedies and unforeseen events

These sons of Mawu also have sons of their own, each governing the respective Vodun facets of their fathers, and so the number of Voduns or spirits multiply, each governing specific aspects or facets of life and the world.

Belief in a Soul

Voodoo practitioners believe in the concept of a soul which can leave the body during dreams and spirit possession. In fact, there is an animistic side to Voodoo in which they believe that inanimate objects and natural phenomena such as rocks, trees, storms, etc., possess souls. These souls - whether human or otherwise, comprise the many Loa which are considered spirits, with whom Voodoo practitioners nurture their connection, and through them, with divinity and the spirit world.

Rituals, Priests and Priestesses

The prominence and authority of the Voodoo priests and priestesses stem from their close connection with the spirits, and the honor and respect accorded to ancestors also yield to hereditary lines of priestesses. Thus they are expected to perform many of the affairs for which people go to the spirits in the first place: healing, advice, and various solutions to life's problems. Voodoo priests and priestesses (Juju man or woman) practice an elaborate system of folk medicinal practices, and they also draw on the wisdom and ethical practices of the past through oral traditions of songs, proverbs, stories, and folklore, many of which have been passed down through generations upon generations. With the aid of the spirits, magic and sorcery are also practiced by Voodoo priests and priestesses.

This asking for help is sometimes accompanied by sacrificial offerings of chicken or sheep or alcohol pouring. In West Africa, human sacrifices ended almost a century ago, so these days, animals are traditionally sacrificed. Some festivals or gatherings are certainly partly or mostly religious. Although the names of these festivals or celebrations and their purposes vary depending on the region and the traditions of the people celebrating them, the essence is the same: spiritual contact with the Voduns and recognizing and celebrating the Vodun's power over matters on earth.

Talismans and Fetishes

Central to any Voodoo culture is a marketplace that sells talisman ingredients called "fetishes." The uses of these talismans or charms (also called "gris-gris") can vary from medicinal to spiritual powers, and a trip to a fetish market can yield an interesting array of ingredients such as stones, dried animal heads, animal parts, or elaborate statues that represent any of the diverse Voodoo gods. Voodoo shrines can usually be seen topped with various Voodoo fetishes, and these shrines would be placed strategically to protect family homes or areas. Food or wine are laid before these shrines as offerings to the Vodun spirits.

Chapter Three. Building Your Voodoo Shrine

You must learn how to construct your own voodoo altar or shrine if you are serious about becoming a Voodoo practitioner and follower. It should be devoted to the ancestor or Lwa you wish to summon regularly. It may seem not easy at first, especially for those who are new to the religion. Still, after you have everything ready, you can learn the fundamentals and finally master how to construct and build your Voodoo shrine.

Types of Altars

The first step you have to take when building your Voodoo shrine or altar is to determine its exact purpose. This will show you the specific type of shrine or altar you have to build. It will guide you to determine the tools and objects you need and the requirements you have to adhere to, especially regarding the positioning and placement of the sacred items.

Here are the different types of altars or shrines you can build:

Ancestor Altar – You can build this one if your goal is to connect with your ancestors. You will be putting pictures of your departed loved ones on the altar. You may also include some items, particularly those they love, to serve as their reminders. It is also advisable to put a plate and cup for food and drink offerings.

Deity Altar – As the name suggests, this altar is meant to worship Lwas, spirits, and deities. You can make this altar a shared space but make sure that the specific spirits and deities you intend to summon permit it. For this altar to work, dedicate a space to leave your offerings. There should also be a space where you can light candles and incense and offer items that the spirit or deity favors. Sometimes, the altar holds idols as a means of standing in for the Lwas or spirits you intend to worship or honor in that space.

Nature Altar – You can also dedicate a space designed to honor nature. In most cases, you can see these altars being filled with things representing the natural elements –seashells and stones. Remember that the nature altar can't be used as a sacred space for your offerings.

Temporary Altar – You can create this type of altar for certain events, like a festival meant to worship or honor a certain Lwa or deity. You can also use it whenever you need to do a certain magical rite. It is meant for rituals and holidays. That it is temporary means, you can dismantle it right after the event.

The specific purpose you intend your altar to perform should be deciding on the type you have to choose.

Finding the Appropriate Space

After deciding on the type of altar or shrine to build, the next thing you should do is to look for the right space where you can set it up. You need enough space so you can comfortably perform the ritual. Some things you can use as your altar or shrine would be:

A Small Table – You may want to use your coffee or end table for your altar. One advantage is that you can easily move it, plus it provides a clean and flat surface capable of holding various things. You can also thrift it conveniently. Just make sure you spend time cleaning the table before using it.

The Top of Your Dresser – If you have an unused dresser at home, you can use the top for your sacred altar or shrine. It is a great idea, especially if you have kids and pets at home since they can't easily reach it. Since it is a dresser, you can put it in a place where people can see right away and interact or communicate every day. It may not be a suitable choice for you, though, if you are uncomfortable setting up your altar or shrine in your room.

Cabinet – You can also use any cabinet you can find at home. It provides adequate space, plus it comes with multiple levels, giving you the chance to pick a level for a specific purpose. If you have only a small space, then you can set aside a bit of space from a desk, bookshelf, or dresser in your home.

However, ensure that even if you're sharing a particular space, avoid allowing items that are not supposed to be in the altar to take the space dedicated for it.

Consider and prioritize privacy, too. Despite having a full closet to accommodate a huge setup for your altar, it will be hard to do your rituals or ceremonies if you display it out in the open. You can put a tiny altar in a closet, which you can close at any time.

Those are just a few examples of items of spaces that you can set aside for your altar or shrine. Remember that your choice serves as an external representation of inner mysteries. It tangibly shows what may happen in your spirits and hearts. This means you have to choose the most suitable space wisely.

Also, the shrine or altar you have built is the key for you to reflect, honor, remember, and heal from grief – anytime you want. It works as your private space – one that lets you reflect, grieve, meditate, honor, remember, and engage in personal rituals with anyone who has departed.

You can also use a small and portable shrine – one you can conveniently carry anywhere you want. It could be an extremely small one, like a matchbook, which can easily fit your pocket. You can also use a bigger one, but you can easily slip into your briefcase or purse.

By choosing a shrine you can carry anywhere, it will be easy for you to maintain the connection you have established with your loved one – even those who have died. It also gives you a sacred space you can use to remember someone or perform a personal ritual regardless of where you are.

What Do You Need for Your Voodoo Altar/Shrine?

Once you already have a space for your altar or shrine, it is time to gather the things necessary for you to make it work for your Voodoo rituals. You may want to put a few things on the altar, such as your magical tools. However, remember that the ultimate goal should be to make the altar as functional as possible. With that in mind, you have to set it up with items to attain your goals.

Some things that include the altar are:

Symbols of four classical elements

These elements are the earth, air, fire, and water. It is crucial to align these elements with the four corresponding cardinal directions. Here, you have to use a bowl containing sand or earth in your altar's north aspect to represent the earth, incense in the east to represent air, water in the west, and charcoal or candle in the south to symbolize fire.

Candles

Your altar should also have candles. It could be a god candle or goddess candle, depending on what your ritual or spell requires. It would also be best to choose different colors for the candles. You may also use candles that represent the four directions. Just ensure that you also have a match or lighter so you can easily light them.

Wand

You may also want to put a wand on your altar. This wand is often helpful in directing energy. Note that the specific way you will be laying this wand and the exact spot where you will be putting it on the altar will greatly depend on what you intend to do, but wise advice is to put it close to or on the altar.

Athame

You can also put an athame on your altar. It refers to a blunt and double-edged blade used in channeling energy. It often has a black handle and blunt blade, which helps prevent accidents during ceremonies and rituals. One thing you should remember about an athame is to prevent yourself from using it for physical cutting. What you have to do, instead, is use it for cutting energy symbolically. With the athame in your altar, you can guide energy every time you do your rituals or ceremonies.

An item that makes your shrine or altar unique from its surroundings – If you set up the altar in a different spot, use a table cover or cloth. It should indicate that the entire space is dedicated to the Voodoo altar or shrine.

If you set it up in a shared space, like the top of your dresser or your work desk, then look for an item that will instantly send a warning that a particular space is only meant for the altar. By doing that, you can maintain the orderliness and cleanliness of that particular spot. It can also prevent you from placing other things that are not supposed to be on the altar.

One thing you can do is to create a small crate or box. It should serve as a shrine. You may also set it up as a tray where you can keep important things on.

A spot where you can put anything you want to offer to the Lwa or ancestor – It could be a small dish or tray. Dedicate it to the offerings so you can easily monitor what you have left in there during the ritual.

A clear space where you can put temporary items – There should be a clear space dedicated to some temporary items you need. It is advisable to put divinatory tools on your altar so that you can bless or charge them right away. Some examples would be certain icons designed to represent specific issues you feel require help. By dedicating a clear space for such a purpose, you can prevent the order of your altar from being untidy.

A personal item so valuable and meaningful to you – You may want to put such things if you want your altar to have some personal effects. By putting something meaningful to you on your altar, you can easily create a channel between the actual practice and you. You may add a painting, idol, a specific incense, or anything that is personal to you and meets your specific needs.

Place any other item you think you need and have the available space for. You may also want to put any components of the spell you need, like ale and cakes. If you plan to use your altar to celebrate a particular event or holiday that specifically points to the Lwa you intend to summon, decorate your altar based on that, too. Ensure that the altar has everything you need to do your rituals effectively.

Building Your Altar

- Once you have chosen the space, the things you need, and the actual altar you will be using, it is time for you to set it up. It is crucial to note that you can create the altar either for a public or private space. The only things you should never forget incorporating into this space are respect and sincerity. Ensure that you also build your altar based on these tips:

- Clean the surface first using a spiritual solution, such as rose water or Florida water. Wipe it dry, then pray aloud to express your desire to make the space and specific surface intended for the altar holy.

- If you are using a table constructed from wooden material, you can bless it using oil, such as ancestor or Van oil. After that, look for a cloth you can use to cover the altar. It is preferable to use white, but you can also be more creative in your cloth choice. Try avoiding synthetic materials and dark colors, though. It would be best to go for cotton then use it to cover the altar.

- Make sure to put beautiful and meaningful objects on the altar. They can be Voodoo dolls, statues, talismans, roots, stones, or flowers. Pick things that have special meaning or those that inspire you. The altar should also contain incense, candles, anointing oils, or perfumes.

- Put water on the altar. Another tip for setting up the perfect Voodoo altar or shrine is to regularly put water on it. It can contribute a lot to gaining more clarity in life. Do not forget to change the water frequently.

- Identify the exact purpose of the altar. You can make it to honor the dead or living, particularly those who have inspired you. If so, then ensure that you put pictures of them on the altar, too.

- Meditate before the shrine or altar you have built every day. This should serve as your daily ritual. When meditating, concentrate on the positive changes you intend to make happen in your life and the lives of your family members, loved ones, and the entire Voodoo community.

In most cases, all Voodoo devotees, even priests, make it a point to build a small altar designed for a certain Lwa in their households. They use these altars or shrines as focal points for their meditation and prayer. It is at this altar or shrine that they perform private devotionals. This private home altar specifically designated for a Lwa is called an *ogantwa.*

This ogantwa holds many items found in hounfo's *badji* (temple room), such as lithographs or exact representations of the spirit or Lwa, satin scarves made of different colors, thunderstones, and dolls. You may also have to put a kind of perpetual lamp here. You can also make a basic ogantwa using a shelf or table or a cabinet. Each is dedicated to a certain Lwa.

To make this ogantwa work for your chosen Lwa, put an image of a saint or spirit. An example is St. Claire, who is a spirit capable of bringing about illumination and clarity. Other examples of images you can use are those of the Holy Virgin, Danbala (St. Patrick), Papa Legba, Papa Ogou (St. George, and Mater Dolorosa (Ezili Freda).

Just like water being important for an altar designed for general or multiple purposes, you also need a bowl or glass of fresh water placed on the ogantwa for it to work. As a devotee, you may need to put a bell or rattle there so you can easily call the spirits. Other items you should put in your shrine are a glass bowl designed for lamp making, olive oil, cotton wicks, white taper candles, and a small brazier you can use for the incense.

Baptize the ogantwa, too. This is the key to cleansing and blessing it before each use. Usually, you will be asked to burn frankincense then recite three prayers, like Our Father or Hail Mary, for a certain period. After that, sprinkle your ogantwa with holy water taken from Catholic churches. This should be enough to baptize the ogantwa. Once done, you can start using it to act as your focal point for meditation and prayer.

Chapter Four.   The Voodoo Doll

A doll has been used to represent someone in many religions. It is referred to as a poppet by several religions, particularly Pagan religions. Regardless of religion, the idea of these toys is essentially the same. The idea for this poppet was more widely employed in British Pagan cults, and it did not originate with Voodoo in Africa.

However, it has become connected with Voodoo through time, owing to popular culture. It is more closely linked with New Orleans Voodoo, and as a result, readymade Voodoo dolls are readily available in stores. These dolls are called sympathetic magic, which is a sort of magic that involves using an effigy containing a personal object from the individual on whom the spell is cast. A lock of hair is one of the most frequent gifts, but you can also use something meaningful to them. After the doll is created, it is no longer just a representation of the person; anything that occurs to the doll might impact the person.

These effigies are also thought to offer the maker a means of communicating with deities. You can then ask them to use their power in this manner. A voodoo doll can be used for an infinite number of things. The method for making your voodoo doll that we shall explain is natural. As a result, you'll only be able to use items that are readily available in nature. This is most likely how the original poppet creators worked. Keep in mind that, when used properly, a voodoo doll can work some serious power. You should not embark on such a project without careful consideration.

How to Create A Voodoo Doll

The first thing you need to do is gather the things you will need to make the doll. You are going to need:

- Strips of cloth

- Some type of natural glue

- Two sticks or branches

- Thread

- Something to put inside the doll, like pine needles or grass

If you would like to dress your doll once it is made, you will also need some buttons, cloth scraps, feathers, and other items to clothe your doll. Since these dolls are supposed to resemble another person, it is a good idea to use things that belong to that person to decorate your doll with. These could be bodily fluids, hair, clothes, and so on. After you have gathered everything you need, you can start to make your doll.

First, take one short and one long stick. Create a cross using the two sticks, ensuring that one in the longer stick appears to be longer than the other end. It should look like a cross. Use the thread to tie the two sticks together using an x-shaped movement across the sticks.

The shorter stick ends will be the doll's arms, and the top or shorter end of the long stick will be the head. The other end of the long stick is the body of the doll.

Whatever you chose to use for stuffing, wrap it around the poles. Begin at the middle where the sticks meet, then move to the head, then the arms, and then down the bottom.

Now you can use some glue to hold this stuff together and place the doll's cloth. You can then use a needle and thread to sew the front and back of the cloth together so that the stuffing doesn't fall out. Many people will also make sure that some of this stuffing can be seen at the ends of the arms, top of the head, and the bottom of the feet.

You can now add a face to the doll. You can use two beads for the eyes and another bead to represent the mouth.

You can dress up the doll now. It is best to use things that belong to the person that the doll is meant to represent. You may also use some of their hair so that the doll is more powerful. The doll is ready and can be used, and you can move onto the next step in the process.

Baptizing The Voodoo Doll

Once you have created the doll, you need to bring it to life. The doll gets baptized using a simple Catholic rite. If you have it available, you can use some holy water. You will say the following:

"I baptize you (name the person) in the name of the Father, the Son, and the Holy Spirit. In life, this is now what you will be. Everything that happens to this doll now happens to (name the person) as I command. As the days pass, only I can control the deepest desires, dreams, and actions of (name the person). Your life is now under my control. (Name the person) will not feel any pleasure unless that's my command."

Where indicated, you will say the person's name out loud.

Properly Using Your Voodoo Doll

Now that the doll has been created and brought to life, you can start to use it to achieve your goals, whatever they may be. You can use the doll in various ways, and we'll go over a few of them now. You have to be very careful when using your doll because it can go awry if you are not careful.

The first use for your voodoo doll could be to make somebody fall in love. This is basically a spell that will use the doll to make a person love you. It will not require any sort of pins or needles or anything of that nature. All you do need is:

- A white candle
- Red marker or pen
- Paper
- 3 pieces of ribbon in black, red, and white
- Something that belongs to you
- Something that belongs to the other person
- A doll to represent the other person

Take the doll representing the other person and take their items, which could be nail clippings, hair, or cloth, and tie them to their doll. Add some of your own elements to the doll.

This is best done during the day after the moon was new. Get everything ready, and then light the candle. Take three ribbons and wrap the doll in them, creating a knot wherever you need to. Say: "Threads that unite and enclasp your heart with mine are intertwined."

Write the name of the other person onto a piece of paper and lay it on your altar. Place the doll over top of the paper and then blow out the candle. The following night, light the candle and then pick up your doll.

Without burning the doll, move its feet close to the flame, say: "Yearn for me. Or burn for me."

Lay the doll back onto the paper. This time, you need to let the candle burn for another 30 minutes. During this time, meditate upon your intentions. Picture your desired outcome and feel all of the emotions connected to it filling you up.

The person you would like to show interested in you will fall in love with you. Once the spell starts to work, wrap the doll up and put it somewhere, it won't be disturbed or harmed so that the spell continues to work

As you are already aware, voodoo dolls are also able to be used to cause damage. Historically, these forms of spells get used for revent. If you create a doll to represent a person that you hate, you can use that doll to inflict severe pain and, possibly, death. You would usually prick the doll with nails or tie it up with a rope for this type of damage. Remember, though, using a voodoo doll for evil purposes can end up having really bad consequences because if you were to lose control, you may end up suffering and possibly dying. It is best if you don't use voodoo dolls for such sinister purposes. Even though Hollywood has sensationalized the negative uses for voodoo dolls, there are just as many positive uses for them. These can be used to call upon good spirits and help bring about a lot of change within the world. You can treat a voodoo doll just like you would a person, asking them to act and respond to how you would like them to.

Pricking various colored pins into them is one of the most common ways to use the doll. Each of the colors will have a different effect.

- White = positive energies
- Black =attraction of negative energies or repulsion
- Pink = death
- Blue = love
- Purple = spirituality
- Green = tranquility
- Yellow = money
- Red = power

Before pins should be used, you need to take time to meditate upon what you are looking to create. For example, if the spell is being performed upon yourself, you can always place a pin into a specific part of your doll. Placing a pin in the heart for emotions, the head would be for knowledge and the stomach for physical sensations.

Making Your Own Voodoo Doll

This means that you would be creating a doll that represents you. When you do this, you can consider all of your own proportions, such as height and figure. You should think about how you view yourself as you create this doll. Once you have created the doll, you can add a bit of your perfume or cologne to the chest, belly, and forehead. You will then chant:

"I baptize you (state your name). Now you and I are one!"

You can then dress up your doll using old clothes. Using an old shirt to create a new shirt for your doll, you can also use some old pants to create pants for the doll. You can also use some of your own hair to place upon your doll's head.

You can now use this doll to perform magic on yourself. You can now perform voodoo spells on yourself. Ensure you get rid of any remnants of supplies that you had left over, such as clothes and hair. You must keep your doll safe. It is best to place it into a box and then hide it somewhere it can't be found. If the wrong person winds up with your doll, they willcontrol your life and you.

Performing Voodoo Magic on Yourself

There are quite a few spells out there that you can use with your doll to help change your appearance. No matter your age, it is always best that you already have some experience performing this type of magic. This way, you will be able to create your own spells with ease.

We'll go over a weight loss spell that you can perform on yourself. To begin, place four candles on a table or altar. You will want two white candles—this help to fill you up with clear energy. One blue candle will help you speak to your mind and body to make sure you receive whatever it is that you want. And a golden candle is going to help with health and give you the power to transform and create.

Light your candle and sit the voodoo doll in the middle of them. Undress your doll and then start to touch your "problem areas" with your finger. Keep in mind; you need it to look like you. Notice how this spot starts to feel warm on your body.

These types of spells work through feelings and being able to visualize what is happening. If you aren't feeling anything, then you are likely not doing everything correctly. Press slowly on the doll until it starts to change. Work to make muscles visible on the doll. You need to change the body into what you want it to look like. Pay attention to how you feel because this is when you will start receiving signals about what you want for yourself. If this is being done correctly, you are going to start feeling a change in your mentality. Eventually, you will start to feel your body losing some weight, that your fat is burning away, and then your life has been changed forever.

Now, if you remain feeling good as you do this spell, you will notice that it is normal for you to feel full of energy and happiness. Once you have finished this ritual, go about your day just you would normally. You have already activated the magic. First, you'll notice that you don't need to eat as much. Secondly, you will notice that you have loads of energy and that you actually want to head out to the gym. Third, this ritual will also help to cause your body to improve your metabolism subconsciously, and it will help you to start losing weight fast than before.

By using your voodoo doll, you can change up the size of your genitals, the length or shape of your legs, or your height. However, it would help if you were extremely careful. If you accidentally break your doll, you could end up unleashing a curse upon yourself.

Another spell you could do for yourself using your voodoo doll is a rejuvenation spell. For this particular spell, you are going to need the participation of another person. You will want them to be the same sex and younger than you. Ask them to hold onto your doll.

You will want to make sure that your assistant is friendly, full of energy, and ready to spread all of that energy with you, and you need to make sure that the assistant isn't going to end up betraying you or break your doll.

Your assistant will hold the doll for five minutes, and that will help you to feel ten years younger. Plus, the spell isn't going to affect the person who is helping. They should not experience any sort of dizziness or weakness.

As for the rest of the spell, you can make it into anything you would like. You can use candles, herbs, stones, music, or anything else you believe relates to fertility and youth.

Use voodoo dolls wisely. Not every ritual or spell in the voodoo religion has to make use of a voodoo doll. In fact, many of them don't use a doll, but if you choose to work with them, be smart and careful.

Chapter Five. Voodoo Queens, Kings, and Loa

Voodoo Queens

Voodoo Queens served in a variety of leadership capacities in religious organizations. While I've already addressed Marie Laveau, the most famous of them all, if you're familiar with her, you'll have a better understanding of what the Voodoo Queens were all about. Queens preside over ceremonial gatherings and direct or perform all ritual dances. At huge group gatherings, they act as ringleaders, attempting to persuade the throng to collaborate towards a single goal. They're the Mojo Bags, charms, blessed amulets and talismans, Gris-Gris, powders, and brews creators and sellers.

They sell charms that are designed to attract a variety of wants, depending on the seeker's intentions. During the time of slavery, strong women paved the road for black power, and they continue to do so now in a similar fashion. Their influence is strong and lasting. After the Embargo Act was enacted in the United States in the 19th century, Voodoo Queens were free black women who purchased the property and established themselves as pillars of society. They were given some rights, and they used them to help the growth of more and more freedom, not just for black women but also for black men and families.

Marie Laveau

Marie Laveau is considered the most powerful Voodoo Queen of them all. She was renowned for offering good advice to respectable men in the community and following through with positive results. She was also respected and honored because of how large and diverse her clientele was. She was the go-to consultant to everyone, from politicians to business people, lawyers, and wealthy investors. However, she never ignored the needy. She would help those who were poor, needy, enslaved, or trapped in any sense. Runaway slaves throughout Louisiana had credited their escape to Miss Laveau and her magical methods. She was a devout Catholic, as well as a Voodoo Queen, and encouraged those who saw her go to church services as a way of protecting and masking their true beliefs from the world. As a result of this, she has been credited for the overlap between Catholicism and Voodoo that has developed since her time.

Laveau was a hairdresser as well and collected her town gossips as she worked. She would then use this insight to impact her city, always working with the laws of nature to procure a more peaceful balance. Her gravesite, located in the oldest cemetery in the state, is now a major tourist attraction and her store located in the French Quarter and her religious site is located on the shore of Lake Pontchartrain. Believers of Voodoo often visit these sites, offering her spiritual gifts to ask for her wisdom and guidance in return. What's more, gamblers shout her name as they place their bets or blow on their dice, and often practitioners will light a candle on her legendary "St. John's Eve". In 1874, over twelve thousand individuals gathered together - both black and white - to watch Marie perform her rites over Lake Pontchartrain on the 23rd of June or St. John's Eve.

Voodoo Kings

Though they did not influence the racial and socioeconomic scene the way the Queens did, Voodoo Kings held high ranking and made a particular impact during their prime reign. One King rose to the ranks above the rest, appearing under Bayou John, Doctor John, and Prince John. John had brought an intense knowledge of Voodoo with him from his home country of Senegal when he was brought over as a slave. At his arrival, he rose quickly through the hierarchy, and because of his deep knowledge, became a leader for others.

Prince Ke'eyama

This Voodoo legend was originally born in Haiti under the name Frank Staten. His family moved him to New Orleans as an infant and raised him under the impression that he descended from African royal blood and that he possessed supernatural abilities of all sorts. Raised by his grandparents, he was taken under the wing by Papa John Bayou at a rather young age.

Prince Ke'eyama settled in New Orleans permanently in the 1970s, where he took on the name Papa Midnight, developed a Chicken Man persona, and performed nightclub acts consisting of magic, dancing, and his infamous bit where he would bite off the head of a chicken and drink its blood. Though he had thousands of followers and his name became famous, many regarded him as more of a showman than a true Voodoo practitioner.

Loa

The Loa stem from all across the lineage of Voodoo. These Loa aid spiritual seekers in differing ways throughout their lives, such as sexuality, spirituality, success, love, visions, and illness. Loa is almost like patron saints in that they represent a particular aspect of life and your service and pray to them for guidance. They are more like guardians, angels, or spirit guides in how they have captured and cultivated particular wisdom and truths in their lifetimes above humanity. They then turn around and attempt to instill this wisdom in those who come to them for aid in life.

Loa are divided into groups, known as Nanchons, or 'nations,' in Voodoo. New Orleans Voodoo is a mixed bag of regions across the globe, and thus there is a subsect of Loa from each of these regions, or 'Nanchons.' Some Loa is more potent than others. Further to the ones I will delve into here, you can also go searching through the patron saints of Christianity as they have fused quite well with those from the regions of Africa and Haiti. Many practitioners pray to saints and Loa, just the same.

Below are some major Nanchons and their defining qualities:

Rada Loa: These Loa are generally older, from the kingdom of Dahomey, Africa. These Loa are water spirits and often prefer to be served with water. These spirits are rather calm, and they are highly revered for their strength and benevolence. Amongst these Loa are Loko, Papa Legba, La Sirene, Marassa, Erzulie Freda, Agwé, Ayizan, Dhamballah Wedo, and Ayida Weddo. These Loa are generally associated with the color white.

Petro Loa: These more fiery Loa can come across as aggressive and combative when they visit. The roots of these Loa extend from Haiti, where they are considered dubious and somewhat mischievous counterparts to the Rada Loa. These Loa are said to have powers of great darkness, where they can damage or negatively affect a situation with the flick of a finger or blink of an eye. Because of this, they are greatly feared. A few infamous petro Loa include 'the master trickster' Met Kalfu and Ezili Dantor. The traditional color for these Loa is red.

Kongo Loa: Marinette, a fierce femme fatale, stems from this region in the Congo and is revered for her feminine prowess. These Loa also include the Simbi Loa, traditionally.

Nago Loa: These Ogoun and Nago Loa originate in Yorubaland and are generally on the gentler side of things.

Ghede Loa: These are the spirits of the dead. Traditionally, the Barons lead the way from this subset of Loa. The Barons include Samedi, Cimitiére, La Croix, Papa Ghede and Kriminel. Maman Brigitte, then, brings the female energy to the fore as a fierce entity of femininity. These spirits, in general, are quite loud and obnoxious yet sexual and playful in nature. They fear no man, as they have been one, and understand the human sensibilities. They will often try to push the envelope at gatherings where they are summoned, showing off by eating spicy foods, drinking a lot, or fulfilling dares. They are most often represented by the colors black and purple.

For rituals, the Loa generally arrive in the space by "mounting a horse," or in other words, by possessing the one performing the ritual. They either enter into the body of the seeker, or they merely enter their consciousness into a union with the seeker. Historically, Voodoo believers called the ritualist a 'ridden chwal', especially when it involved an individual writhing on the ground or flailing their limbs.

Some of the Loa will arrive in full form, displaying particular behaviors to show their arrival. They make their presence known either through particular actions, phrases, or an overarching demeanor. During their visit, they will generally showcase their character and offer any warranted advice while the seeker feeds them, serves them wine, and treats them as they most prefer to be treated. This is their payment, of sorts, for their efforts. One person takes on a houngan or mongo role and is then in charge of ensuring the Loa is both happy and satisfied and easygoing upon exit. Sometimes the spirits don't want to leave and wish to stay to enjoy the delights of very human existence for a much longer time.

Below find a list of some of the most popular Loa that Voodoo practitioners pray to:

Ayida: The goddess of rainbows, Ayida serves as the primary wife to Dhamballah. The two will often appear in the skies as entwined snakes during the ritual. She is attracted most to the color white and thus loves to be gifted with such goods. Examples include cotton, milk, eggs, rice, and chicken. Ayida serves as the goddess of fertility. Ayizan is her daughter, serves as the goddess of the marketplace, and holds the keys to sacred wisdom and truthful vessels. Ayizan is the head Mambo or priestess of Voodoo.

Marinette: A demi-goddess who sacrificed a black pig to start off the First Haitian Revolution when she was in human form. She, hereafter, died trying to fight for the revolution and was named a demi-god as a result. She is now the patron of slavery and liberation and can either trap an individual or free them from the binds that keep them where they are. Whenever a seeker calls for Marinette, they are urged to either sacrifice a black pig or black rooster or serve one or the other as a meal. Once she possesses a human body, she likes to get a little crazy, causing fits of anger or violent thrashing. Marinette is the protector of werewolves, and she holds owls in an austere reverence; they are her familiars.

Kalfu: The deity of sorcerers, Kalfu rules the night and reigns over the moon. He rules over much black magic and holds lordship over destruction, poor luck, charms, and injustices. Black eyes and tears are sure to show whenever Kalfu is present in a circle, as he loves to drink rum laced with black gunpowder and play with those he inhabits. He stands as the dark counterpart to Legba. Where Legba is light, he is dark.

Zaca: Standing as the patron of field and farm workers, Zaca rules over the harvest and all of agriculture. He is wise, friendly, and sweet-tempered. As one of the most approachable of the Loa, many fondly call him 'cousin Zaca.' He appears in fields and farmland - the lands he loves - and usually enjoys smoking a pipe and drinking rum while casually holding a machete. Generally, Zaca will dress in denim clothing with a straw hat and be especially active in social circles around his holy day, which falls on Haitian Labor Day (1st of May).

Loco: The patron deity of Voodoo priests and doctors, Loco reigns as the god of the wild mother and her wild vegetation in its utmost bounty. He covers a wide spectrum, ranging from healing fruits and herbs to harmful ingredients meant to injure. Goddess Ayizan is Loco's wife.

Loco discovered the god Nibo when he was just a stone wrapped up in a swaddling cloth. After taking the stone home with care in his heart, the stone turned into a real child - that of Nibo. Ogun serves as godfather to Nibo, and Nibo has since ruled as the god of cinnamon and as one of the death gods, or Ghede.

Legba: Often the first god to be invoked in any Voodoo rituals, Legba holds rank as the sun god, as well as the veil that stands between humanity and the gods. It's no wonder why he speaks every human language, as he is actively a transmuter and translator of sorts between humans and the other Gods. All Gods must go through Legba to travel between realms, and as such, he is the gatekeeper. The land of the Gods is known as Guinee, and Legba holds the key to that terrain. By extension, he also holds over all gates and crossroads, exists as the light to Kalfu's darkness. The two are yin and yang to one another and coexist to maintain balance. Legba crafts quite the image when he appears on his cane, having a straw hat, pipe, and aging skin and body. Legba holds all dogs as sacred and individual.

Maman Brigitte: One of the most powerful gods of death [one of the thirty Gods of Ghede], Brigitte is quite a foul-mouthed little lass. She is the goddess and wife to Baron Samedi and focuses her efforts guarding cemetery graves, especially when topped with rocks. She rules over unfulfilled justices and prefers to be served hot peppers and rum, in line with her fiery soul and sizzling persona. Whenever a Voodoo cemetery is formed, a figure of Maman Brigitte is buried in the first grave as a symbol of her presence and protection from disturbing forces.

Ogun: God of fire, war, iron, metalworks, technology, and political matters, Ogun is often referred to as the Hercules of Voodoo. It is presumed amongst most Haitians that Ogun battles in every war, fighting for the people under a human disguise. He is often represented by a sword stuck in the earth, victorious and humble. When Ogun possesses an individual, the human form will withstand burning temperatures and will generally wash their hands in fuming burning sugar cane as an attempt on Ogun's behalf to encourage trust and faith. The hands never burn. Ogun craves rum but asks for it oddly, as a trick, and will often announce "my testicles are cold" broadly, with the desire of drinking fresh in his mind.

After becoming Nibo's godfather, Ogun decided to adopt him, thus initiating a rivalry between Nibo and his own son, Ogubadagri. Fights are often formed in circles with disputing supporters, as the emotions are still solid.

Agwe: The god of the ocean, the sea, and ruler of plant and animal sea life, Agwe was the one who taught men and women how to build boats fit for the ocean and how to fish for food. He also serves as the patron of anglers and sailors. Agwe is usually presented with his gifts in the ocean, often in the form of a boat filled with gifts and holes, which cause the boat to sink and present Agwe with his gifts. Agwe dresses as a naval officer and is known for his oceanic green eyes. He is one of the husbands of Erzulie, the goddess of love, and he spends most of his time living in an overarching plantation found deep in the sea.

Agwe rules over some other deities including Labaleen, goddess of whales; Adjassou, goddess of spring water; Clermeil, god of the river and floods.

Erzulie: Goddess of love, passion, and beauty, Erzulie always wears three wedding rings to showcase her ties with each of her husbands: Dhamballah, Ogun, and Agwe. The three men truly adore and lavish her. They treat her like the goddess she is and try to help her through her suffering due to all the human heartbreak she represents. When she appears in a circle, she most often requests a glass of pink champagne, perfumes, powders and makeup, sugar cakes, and all things decadent. Erzulie is not a loyal partner by any means and often loves too many men to avoid affairs with men that aren't her husbands. However, she absolutely refuses to be with Nibo, as he is overall darker than she can handle.

Dhamballah: One of the more infamous deities, this serpent god created living beings, created the other gods and deities, encircles the earth, and manages all life force energy and intelligence. His wife is the goddess Ayida, and they are, as I mentioned before, often shown as entwined together. When not with her, he resides among the Sacred Tree, living humbly within its branches. This snake god takes care of young children, the elderly, and the decrepit or deformed. He loves and nurtures those who are too different from being accepted, as he feels responsible, as their creator. He requests and adores precious silver metal makings of all kinds and helps in exchange by connecting humans with their earthly desires. Those possessed by him will hiss, snake style, rather than speak in words. Simbi, Dhamballah's son, rules over the rain and is represented as a white snake god.

Baron Samedi: Wife of Maman Brigitte, Baron Samedi is one of the most popular Loa and is the head of the Ghede, or death gods. Often, this god will fall on the floor, then expecting the practitioners to dress him up in his infamous garb, including a formal overcoat with tails, a top hat, white skeleton makeup, and cotton plugs in his nostrils (to help guard him against the stench of constant human death that occurs in our realm). He speaks in a nasal tone and is well known for causing quite the ruckus, whenever he visits the human realm. He is most fond of rum, tobacco, debauchery, and disruption and is the gatekeeper, guarding the veil that sits between life and death. He rules over resurrection and decides who to heal and who to help move onward whenever he is called upon to offer his services. He will surprise you, no doubt, and he may be a tricky one to get rid of, especially if he ends up taking a fancy to a woman present. He is fond of human life, craves the taste, and loves the chase. He is the master of the crossroads between life and death and greets all souls before leading them down to the underworld.

Chapter Six.   Invocation and Summoning Ritual

Invocation and summoning rituals are two of the most important parts of the Voodoo religion. These rituals are designed to summon a specific Lwa based on the occasion or the specific intention of the Voodoo practitioner performing the ceremony. The close connection between the dead and the living is one of the fascinating aspects of Voodoo. Life itself gives birth to Lwas and spirits, which the followers must summon according to their objectives.

Contrary to popular belief, invoking or summoning spirits does not always imply that you are summoning the evil ones. You can also call on benevolent spirits such as deities, ancestors, and gods and goddesses to help you. You can do so by saying earnest prayers and responding in a nonviolent manner.

Music and chanting should always be present while invoking and summoning a certain spirit or Lwa. Dance rhythms, music, and chanting are more appealing to the spirits because it demonstrates how the devotees worship, honor, and respect them.

Music and chants, as well as earnest prayers, are required to address the spirit with respect. With this incorporated, you have a better possibility of successfully bringing the spirit to life and allowing them to direct you in your daily activities.

The act of summoning and invoking spirits is a form of magic that is considered sophisticated. The reason for this is that it necessitates the summoning of a higher being in the form of a spirit or Lwa, as well as a deity. With that in mind, you should never take this procedure for granted. If you're summoning a creature or spirit that doesn't want to be summoned gently, don't do it carelessly.

If you want to summon a high-frequency spirit or entity, make sure you do your homework first. In this situation, frequency refers to the vibratory level at which an entity or spirit acts.

Importance of Purpose and Intention

Aside from music and chanting that serve as avenues to show respect to the Lwas, it is also necessary for you to have a distinct intention or purpose for summoning and invoking a Lwa. As a beginner, you have to know exactly your purpose or intention for summoning a spirit. There should be a distinct goal or purpose in mind. Knowing your exact purpose will be easier for you to strengthen your skills and focus on your attempt or the entire ritual.

Also, remember that the Lwa you are trying to summon will most likely listen if you can draw their attention to your presence. The invocation's actual purpose will also clearly show you the exact Lwa you should call upon. You can summon a specific spirit or Lwa for purposes like wealth, relationships, health, and social status. You can also invoke one to help you handle a certain problem.

Ensure that you have a good and valuable reason for summoning the spirit. Imagine them as grumpy people who do not want to be disturbed when asleep. With that said, your reason should be really good for calling upon them. You need not be in a life-or-death situation when doing so, but your purpose should be a good excuse to bother and wake them up. Only summon them when you require their help and assistance for a problem you can't solve independently.

How to Invoke or Summon the Right Lwa

To invoke the correct spirit or Lwa, you have to look for a summoning ritual specifically intended for them. You can learn some rituals and magic spells from books and other sources. You can also design and make your own. When choosing or creating rituals, remember that it often consists of three basics steps – building the most suitable atmosphere for the ritual, getting into the trance state, and summoning/invoking and interacting with the spirit.

Create the Perfect Atmosphere

Building the perfect atmosphere for your rituals should be one thing you have to do when invoking Lwas. If you are still new to this realm, you may wonder why rituals often look kind of sinister and scary. This is because it builds up the right atmosphere that encourages the spirits to come out.

This first step aims to create a specific atmosphere in the area designated for the ritual. It is also crucial for the participants of the ritual to have the right mindset. You have to create a mindset of uniformity, self-sacrifice, and discipline and show it in the way you dress for the ritual and set up the designated place for it.

Now, the question is, what kind of atmosphere should you aim for when performing invocation and summoning rituals? The answer is an atmosphere capable of separating you from your mundane daily reality. You have to be in a different atmosphere – one that can convert your mind into a more spiritual state.

Getting Into the Trance State

The atmosphere you have created for the ritual should be the one that will bring you to the right trance state. Here, you will need to use the right sounds, objects, colors, and patterns to connect with your spiritual nature. Reaching the trance state, in this case, does not mean you must get rid of your sense of reality completely.

What you should be after is a theta brainwave state – one like you usually enter as you are falling asleep. It refers to the quiet area between being awake and experiencing your dreams. You have to penetrate this state as this is the most appropriate mental state for spell casting and conjuration.

For you to reach this state of mind, you can use one or a combination of these tools:

Veves/Sigils – The veves or the Voodoo symbols we have discussed in one chapter of this book should be used to get into the trance state. Veves refer to the symbols of various spirits as previously discussed. Used for centuries, you can use them for your summoning rituals by looking directly at them.

You can draw the veve yourself while the ritual is ongoing. Drawing it on your own is beneficial as it can give you a more trance-inducing experience, increasing your chances of getting into the desired trance state fast.

Enns – These refer to sound frequencies that one can use when connecting with spirits and deities. You can chant these *enns* or use them as silent mantras. You may use them based on your discretion, provided the end result is the trance state.

Candles – You also need to have candles around. This is crucial as you need to gaze at the flames of the candles to build a theta state. The reason is that it will let you focus your attention on the flame while also feeling relaxed. Another way to use the candles is to visualize the specific spirit you intend to invoke or summon. Just imagine this spirit manifesting in the flame, and you will have an easier time entering the trance state.

Some Pointy Objects – Some examples are sword, dagger, and wand. They often serve as extensions of your hand. This is necessary as extending your hand will let you channel energy more effectively. It is like that scenario of you hitting someone using any of the mentioned objects.

However, the major difference is you do not use the objects for fighting or combat. What you do, instead, is charge a specific space or object by sending magical energy to it. You can charge a veve or sigil, magical circle, mirror, or anything that symbolizes the spirit you summon or invoke.

Magic Circle – Sometimes, you may need to create a magic circle on the floor. You can mark a circle on the floor, which serves as the exact spot where you can trap the spirit you summon. You may also use this magical circle to protect where you stand or sit while you let the spirit linger or stay outside.

If you plan to use this element for your summoning rituals, remember that it usually requires you to make two circles. One should be for you, while the other should be for the spirit. The good thing about the circle is that it can create a form of separation.

It is great as the spirits may interfere with all the present energies in the area and people. Note, however, that using a magic circle is optional. A lot of those who regularly summon Lwas do not even use this element in their rituals.

Meditation – You can also meditate to reach the trance state. One advantage of this technique is that you do not have to prepare ritual objects for it. The only things you need to reach the trance state through meditation are concentration and a clear mind. Meditate for around thirty minutes to cleanse your mind and get rid of all unnecessary thoughts, making it possible for you to reach the trance state quickly.

Using any or a combination of these tools and techniques, you can bring your mind into a trance-like state, making it possible for you to gain better results from the ritual. You may also use other items, like magic robes, gemstones, and crystal balls. The color of the items also matters a lot. For instance, you can use the color red to invoke warlike spirits. The goal is to use the elements with their corresponding elements and colors to create a trance-inducing state and an appropriate ritualistic atmosphere.

Invoking the Spirit

Now that you have prepared the perfect atmosphere for the ritual and reached the trance state, you can invoke the spirit or Lwa. The state you are in will make it easier for you to interact with spirits. This is mainly because your consciousness is already at that point where you can respond more effectively to such influences. Your goal is to invoke or summon the spirit in such a way it enters your body, allowing you to have its traits.

Avoid mistaking invocation for possession, though, as the two are different. If you are possessed, then it means that the spirit controls you. Invocation, on the other hand, leaves you in control. However, you will have many personality changes since you are already receiving the traits of your summoned spirit.

There, you should start calling for your chosen spirit. You can do it by saying formal incantations from various sources or writing your own rituals and using them. If you are gifted, then you can also rely on any form of inspiration that comes to you during the entire procedure.

It would be best for you to be more creative in your rituals as spirits prefer them. Ensure that you also make the entire ritual a unique and personal experience for you. Once you have successfully summoned the spirit, remember that you can command it. Avoid the mistake of humbling yourself too much. It would not be a great idea to act like a servant or slave when communicating what you want.

Command the spirit as you are a conjurer. You are the creator or god of the entity you have summoned to this plane of reality. Avoid disrespecting the spirit, though. You can command it while still acting with respect, not only to the spirit but also to yourself.

Once you have successfully communicated your desire and got what you want, feel free to end the ritual. What you should do is to thank the spirit. Express how thankful you are for their presence, giving you answers to your questions and providing guidance. Ensure that the candles you light up during the ritual continue burning until they go out independently. After that, you can dispose of them. Avoid reusing the candles or any other items you have used for this ritual for another.

Basic Invocation Ritual

Now that you are aware of the usual steps for invoking spirits, you can follow a basic ritual.

Things You Need:

Silver or white candle

Gift for the spirit – You can offer anything as a gift, but you have to make sure that it fits and represents the spirit you wish to summon. Some great examples are drink, food, and tobacco.

- 1 cup of salt
- Sage smudge stick

Spirit Invocation Instructions:

Get rid of all the negative energies surrounding you. A wise tip is to prepare a cleansing bath. Just run lukewarm water in a tub, then add the salt to it. Soak your body in it for 20 minutes or so. After that, dry off, then wear something comfortable.

Cast a circle and ask for blessings.

Light the sage. Then smudge yourself as well as the area inside the circle. It is helpful to remove the negative energies still there. Allow the sage to continue burning after that.

Put the silver or white candle in a holder. After that, put your offerings or gifts around it.

Close your eyes, then breathe deeply. Your goal should be to focus more on being welcoming and open with your eyes closed and while taking deep breaths. Light the candle, then recite your prepared incantation or ritual.

Wait for the spirit to come to you. If you have successfully summoned the spirit, then ask your questions or request guidance or any other form of help you are seeking.

Invoking Papa Legba

Here is also an example of summoning a specific Lwa in the Voodoo community. In this case, it would be Papa Legba, who you should invoke first as he is the gatekeeper of the spiritual world. It would be best if you knew exactly how you could summon Papa Legba, as he will be the one to open the gates for the spirits to come to you.

Here's what you will need for this invocation ritual:

- Red and black candle
- Rum
- Three coins
- Cigar
- Sugarcane juice
- Cookies and other sweets
- Groundnuts
- Veve of Papa Legba

Procedure:

Put everything on the altar, then light all the things that have to be lit, like the red and black candle and the cigar. Begin meditating.

If you feel ready, summon or call Papa Legba. One great thing about summoning Papa Legba is that language will never be an issue. Do not worry about whether Papa Legba understands you. Summon him by reciting or singing his prayer.

"Papa Legba, open the gate for me. Antibon Legba, please open the gate. Legba opens the gate for me, and I will thank the Lwa when I return."

Observe his response. If you feel like he is already around, you can ask for his help and guidance. Communicate with him, just like when talking to a friend. He will listen to whatever you want to say. Allow yourself to open up to him. After that, ask him respectfully to open up the gates so the other Lwas or spirits will come out. Be specific when mentioning the Lwa you intend to talk to.

After you send your request, offer him the items you have prepared on the altar. This should also be the perfect time to begin invoking the specific Lwa you wish to interact with. Remember, though, that each Lwa requires a different ritual. The reason is these spirits have different preferences.

Once you have completed your invocation rituals to your desired Lwa, express your gratitude to Papa Legba. Thank him for listening to you and allowing you to speak to a specific spirit. Then ask Papa Legba to close the gate as he returns to his world.

After completing the ritual, it would be best to gather all the offerings you have prepared. Bring them to a crossroad so you can drop off Papa Legba together with the gifts you offer him. Leave the offerings beneath a tree close to the crossroad or at the side.

Some Warnings to Keep in Mind

Regardless of what you are looking for, whether it's answers to questions, guidance, or help with any aspect of your life, you have to use the invocation ritual with caution. Do extensive research before you even start. Avoid rushing the process so you prevent mistakes that will lead to irreparable harm to you or anyone. Remember that while this activity is rewarding, it also has consequences if you do not do it correctly.

Chapter Seven. Health Rituals

Everybody desires to be healthy. A good and fulfilling life is built on the foundation of excellent health. Although all human bodies have a similar structure, we are all incredibly different. As a result, such broad advice will not benefit everyone in the same manner. What is beneficial to one individual may be harmful to another. Having the correct attitude is the foundation for excellent health. The best voodoo spells method will start with a correct diagnostic and finish with appropriate activities. It's critical to figure out what's causing the ailment or problem. The sickness will return if you solely focus on the symptoms. Symptoms will go away if you can locate the source of the problem. Organs and processes are interrelated and impact one another, making the human body more complicated than we imagine. As a result, it's critical to identify effective health spells that look at the mind and body as a whole, rather than just the ailment in one part of the body.

However, these miraculous treatments should only account for half of everything you do to improve your health. They should be complemented with traditional medical therapies as well.

Healing Ritual

This is a ritual that actually has Hungarian roots. This gets used when other ways have failed. It uses a lot of eggs. The egg represents a mysterious essence of regeneration and life. We are going to use the power of the egg to help get rid of an illness. This is best performed during a full moon.

You are going to need:

- 13 fresh eggs
- Salt

To start with, you will create a circle using salt. The person who is ill will lie within the circle. The best way to do this is to make sure they are lying on the ground as the moonlights them up. This will increase the magical power.

As they lay there, you will roll an egg across the body of the ill person. Make sure you reach every part of them, front, back, and sides. As you do this, make sure the ill person is praying or saying mantras without stopping. For the best results, the ill person should be completely naked or as close to naked as possible. Of course, you should use your common sense. You don't want a person who is already sick, naked, outside, in the winter. Once you have finished rolling one egg all over their body, place it inside of a bowl.

Do this will all 13 eggs. Once you have used the last egg, the ritual is over. The eggs will absorb the illness, so you should take them away. You can wash them out with running water, or you can break them into a hole in the ground and cover them up. You can also call upon a voodoo deity to help make the ritual stronger.

Good Health Ritual

This spell will use a voodoo doll. You should also make sure you know where the person's illness originated from.

You are going to need:

- Cloth and ingredients for creating the voodoo doll – get hair or fingernails from the ill person if at all possible

It is best to use white fabric to create the doll. You should try to do this spell during the waning moon and to make sure you have complete concentration while performing the spell.

First off, you need to create the actual doll and do your best to make it look like the person. You can use the method of making the voodoo doll that we used in the voodoo doll chapter if you would like. Once the doll has been made, you will call upon Ghedes and Loco. Then you will blow into the nose and mouth areas of the doll. To bind the sick person to the doll, call out their name three times and then baptize it. The baptism is just like what we covered in the voodoo doll chapter. For best results, try to use hair or fingernails from the stick person to create the doll.

Once the doll has been animated, picture how you are going to solve the situation and their illness by making the disease separate from the patient and moving into only the doll. Then take a nail and drive it into the point of the doll where the disease started in the ill person. This will keep the disease in the doll.

After you know that the spell has started to work, you should bury the doll or put it into flowing water.

Healing Stone

This spell is meant to help relieve problems from physical ailments. This comes from old traditions and works on the principle of moving the disease or problem to a non-living object. In the past, people often believed that they could move their issues to an animal. For example, if they rubbed a toad over their body, their warts would go away. Don't worry though; we won't be using any toads. All you are going to need is a stone. The best place to find your stone is near a body of water, like a river, because a smooth, oval, white stone works best.

You are going to need:

- Whitestone
- White thread about 2 feet long
- A needle
- A piece of linen that is big enough to wrap your stone
- Matches
- White tea-light
- Nail

The best time to do this is on a Monday during a waning moon.

Start by visualizing a giant white cross. This cross should be so big that it fills your entire room. Then, pick up the nail and carve a cross symbol into the tea-light candle so that the candle's wick is in the middle of the cross.

As you light the candle, say: "Sick things are now burning, and disease is waning."

Create a small bag from the piece of linen. Fold the linen in half, take the needle and thread, and stitch both sides of the linen.

Next, pick up the stone and touch the areas of the body where you are suffering from a disease or problem. As you do this, picture how all of your problems are moving out of your body and into the stone as gray smoke. Continue to do this until you feel that you have done it for long enough. As you are doing this, you can say:

"As the moon is waning, my disease is disappearing and moving into this stone. I am getting better and better. I am regaining my powers more and more."

Make sure you feel those words as you say them. Concentrate on the feelings of relief and joy that you are getting rid of your disease and are once again healthy.

Once you have finished, place the stone inside of the bag and then toss it into a natural and flowering water source.

Spell for Healing Sorrows

This is meant to burn away bad emotions or sorrows. This spell helps to support you to solve your problems magically. Make sure you remember spells like this; you can't solve all of your problems. In the end, if you are feeling extremely sad and this spell doesn't seem to help, then you may need to meet with a medical professional to get more help. This spell can help you to name the problem and to focus on the solution.

You are going to need:

- The dried hull from five oranges
- Yarrow and dry mint
- Paper
- Quill and red ink
- Tea-light candle
- Lighter or matches
- Dry wood for a fire

You need to make sure that you have a quiet place to perform this outside. It is best done after sunset and during the waning moon.

Start by creating yourself a magic circle, and then create a bonfire using the dry wood. Ensure that you have a safe place for the fire and that it won't catch anything on fire.

Start by visualizing across in bright white light. Next, light your tea-light candle and then, on your paper, write down all of the problems that you are feeling right now. Pick up your dried mint and toss it into the fire. As you do so, say: "I am clearing you away." Then pick up the yarrow and toss it into the fire. As you do, say: "I am free now."

Then toss in the paper with all of your problems written on it. Then toss in the dried orange hulls. As you do, say: "Only sweetness remains; my sorrow is away." Watch the first until it has gone out completely. Once it has burned out, you should bury the ashes as far away from your home as you can.

Healing Energy Spell

This will help to support the healing process and provide energy to your body's problem areas. This spell will help speed up the process of healing without any complications. Make sure that you do not skip modern medicine. You should always follow the doctor's orders. The smartest thing to do is to use all available means to help yourself heal.

You are going to need:

- A small plate or bowl
- Something that is sharp and has a point
- A sacrifice, such as fruit, nuts, or something sweet
- Matches
- Two blue candles

The best time for you to do this ritual is on a Monday during a waning moon.

Start out by creating a magic circle. Pick up one of your blue candles and, using something sharp, carve the name of a Loa or

God, for example, Loco. On the second candle, carve out the name of the ailing person.

Light both of your candles, and then ask the healing powers for help. Offer them the sacrifice you have chosen. Then take a moment to pray for the health of the person that is sick. Visualize them as strong as they could possibly be. The person is now healed and happy that they are full of health and power once more.

Allow the candle to burn for some time to create a pool of wax on the top of the candle. Pick up the first candle and pour that wax into the bowl. Then pick up the second candle and pour this into the bowl. As you do so, say: "As the wax from both candles become one, the healing power of (name God) and the energy of (name of the sick person) become one."

Wait until that wax has solidified. While the wax is still warm, take it out of the bowl and touch the areas of the body where there is a disease or problem. Picture how all of the healing energy from the wax moves into the body.

Once you feel you have done this for long enough, you may end your ritual and close out your circle. Allow these candles to burn out completely. Once they are burned out, they go out into nature and then bury the wax. Release everything and then let the higher forces take over and improve the sick person's health.

Chapter Eight.   Spiritual Cleansing

Let's put magic out of the equation for a while and focus on the emotional, mental, and psychological benefits of taking a bath. It has an uplifting effect on the mind when you get home after a long, hard day and soak in a bath with your favorite soaps and smells, regardless of your gender. You may amp up the effect of a cleansing bath on your spirit and even your physical well-being by using herbs imbued with unique properties.

Purification Baths: Symbolism and Application

Purification baths are meant to purify you for the ritual you want to perform and open you up spiritually to create a channel that allows you access to the spirit world, where you can make your petition known. By doing so, purification baths increase the chances of your desires becoming a reality. But beyond opening you up, a purification bath serves other purposes, and I want to talk about a few of these right now.

Severing Ties:

Some of us unwittingly get ourselves into sticky situations, either through love ties, ancestral curses, or as a result of our actions. One of the many ways to get rid of such a tie is to undergo a purification bath. It helps to separate you from that person, curse, or consequence. When it comes to soul ties, you may come across an individual who is unnaturally addicted to you. Their obsession with you might have negative repercussions in your life. Even if they are not doing anything spiritual, the fact that you may have had some kind of physical interaction with them, whether through intercourse or some other shared intimate activity, may have created a tie with that person without you realizing it. These bonds can become dangerous, especially when the person becomes obsessed with you. As for the ancestral curse, there are times when the sins of the father are visited on the son, so just because you were born to this particular individual could mean that you carry some pain and hurt in your present life due to that lineage. There are special baths that you can prepare to break such a tie and make sure that it ends permanently. Finally, when you offend someone, and that person holds a grudge against you, if they are the spiritual type, they could engage in declarations, sometimes through incantations and spells, that will negatively affect you. Putting yourself through a purification bath will separate you from those declarations and free you from the consequences.

For Protection:

As you ascend in your journey as a Voodoo practitioner, you will realize that a lot of the things we deal with daily are more spiritual than they are physical. The energy that people project towards you can affect you without you even realizing it. The spaces that you inhabit are not entirely new, as they belonged to previous owners. These people may have left a very negative aura in that space. If you do not perform a purification bath, you will find yourself absorbing some of that negativity in different areas of your life.

A purification bath helps to give you additional protection against these unpredictable elements. We can never predict the intentions of another, but a purification bath will protect you from them. Think of it as boosting your immune system. You might not yet be sick, but by feeding your body with the right vitamins and nutrients, you arm yourself against any disease that may want to invade your body. There may not currently be any spiritual attack or negativity in your physical space in the same way. Still, to maintain that serenity and ensure that you are well-guarded against any future attacks, a purification bath will create a barrier that keeps such things out.

For Attraction:

Anything with the ability to repel the negative can also attract the positive, so if you are preparing yourself to attract certain events in your life, a purification bath is a good idea. With the right ingredients, you can use your body as a channel that attracts the kind of things you want to see in your life. There are stones and other elements that can be used for this very purpose in the preparation of a purification bath. If you are able to follow through on some of the rituals diligently, I will share shortly, and you can make yourself a magnet for wealth, love, or even luck. The impact of attraction spells that call for purification baths is greater than simply manifesting what you desire. You can also attract positive energy so that you find yourself constantly associating with the people that you need in your life. When performing a ritual of this sort, the main thing to remember is to ensure that your mind is clear and focused on what you want.

Internal Cleansing

The practice of carrying out an internal body cleanse has more to do with ensuring that you are in a better position to invoke or conjure the things you want. I use the word "cleanse" because it's something that many of us can relate to, but the appropriate term is purification. As you continue to learn more on this journey, you will find that the word "purification" will expand to accommodate concepts like anointing, blessing, and consecration. An internal body cleanses the ingestion of certain mixtures and concoctions explicitly designed for this process. The herbs used in these mixtures are meant to intensify your psychic connection and provide clarity of thought so that you can focus your mind and zero in on the specific thing about which you want to consult with your ancestors.

Finally, you should know that doing an internal cleanse is not solely reliant on ingesting herbs. There are crystals and other curios you might be able to use for such purposes. You can light a candle in some spells and use the power of visualization to draw in the energy you need for an internal cleanse. I usually tell my beginner students that this is a better route to take unless you work with an experienced Hoodoo doctor. The practice of Hoodoo is relatively safe, but you mustn't take this for granted by disregarding basic instructions. You might end up in a far worse situation than what brought you there initially or attract the wrong kind of energy into your life. I share these warnings because the practice of Hoodoo is not a hobby or to be engaged in on a whim. It requires dedication, devotion, and due diligence.

Keeping Negative Energy Away

Many of us need to maintain a personal space filled with positive energy. This is why I feel like the perfect introduction to a purification bath is meant to repel negative energy. In this segment, I will teach you how to create your purification bath using some of the more common herbs, like those I listed earlier and a few others you will need to obtain. I will also walk you through the step-by-step process of completing this ritual. As you continue to practice this, you will absorb more spiritual insight and guidance on some other necessary steps you can take to create unique results in different situations. But for now, let us fill your space with positive energy that will allow you to thrive spiritually and that will create a more enabling environment for your spells to work.

Duration:

This ritual takes place over three days, so make sure you arrange your schedule to work without interruption. I would recommend that you do this once a month or once every quarter, depending on your experiences and personal needs. The first bath is meant to happen just after sunset. It is believed that this is the period that negative forces begin to assemble.

The first ritual will be made up of bitters herbs that repel the activities and intentions of negative spirits towards you.

The second bath is meant to be performed just before dawn, and it is meant to attract positive energy.

The third bath is much like the second, and its sole purpose is to reinforce your intentions from that second bath. It acts as a seal for the attraction magic you are trying to create.

Preparation:

For the first ritual and the first bath on the first day, you will need the following:

- Dandelion roots
- Yarrow
- Wormwood
- Nettle
- Red or purple colored petals
- Horehound
- Vinegar
- Ammonia

It doesn't matter if the herbs used are fresh, dried, or powdered. Remember that this is not a sexy bath situation, so don't try to do the whole spa-like treatment. Start by setting the hot water in the bathtub at a hot but not so hot temperature that it scares you, then add the herbs and petals into the hot water. Add 1/2 cup of vinegar and a few drops of ammonia, and you are set.

For the second and third day of the week will you will need the following:

- Angelica
- Chamomile
- Hyssop
- Allspice
- Comfrey leaves
- Powdered Nutmeg
- Powdered Cinnamon
- White petals
- Honey
- Milk
- Egg

Again, the herbs used here can be fresh, dried, or powdered. You can throw in some whole nutmegs in addition to the powdered nutmeg and cinnamon if you have them. The milk should be three cups, and one egg is enough. I should also point out that you have to prepare the herbal mixture from scratch on the second and third days. Do not use leftovers!

Process:

Day 1: When the time is right, begin by filling the tub with hot water. Then take two candles (preferably white) and place them on opposite ends to act as a doorway to the bath. You will walk through this doorway to enter into the bath when it is ready. Next, pour the herbal mixture into the water along with the ammonia and vinegar, remove your clothing and enter the doorway you made with the candles. If you are using fresh or dried herbs, you can place them in an organza bag to prevent your tub from clogging. If you are a woman on your period, do not take this bath. Blood interferes with the magic. Wait until it's over before you engage in this ritual. Once you are in the water, focus your mind on whatever negative circumstances you are going through and imagine your desire's positive outcome. Completely immerse yourself in the bathwater.

Dunk yourself in the water at least seven times. Do not ingest the contents of this water. Each time you emerge, spend a few minutes meditating on the positive outcome that you desire in your life. If you are in a situation where you are attached to something negative, like bad debts, a bad relationship, or just bad experiences that happened to you, use these meditation moments to detach yourself emotionally from those feelings. By the seventh time you emerge, the water should begin to feel cooler. Step out of the tub through the doorway that you created with the candles. Take a cup and scoop the contents of this water. Set it aside and drain the rest. Do not dry yourself. Allow the water and herbs to seep into your skin so that the magic can work. When you feel dry enough, put on your robe, take that cup of water that you extracted and go outside. Turn your face towards the West, hold the cup over your head and say these words:

"Whatever hold the negative forces or spirits have over me has been broken. I am free from every negative bond. As I cast this water over my head, I am also casting out every negative spirit and energy in my life."

After reciting these words, toss the water out and go back inside. You are done for the night.

Day 2 and Day 3:

Cleanliness is a requirement for these next two rituals, so you must take a personal bath before starting. Also, ensure that the bathtub you use is very clean. Once you have done this, you can start the process by running hot water in the tub and lighting the candles to create an entryway. Next, crack the egg and drop it in the water before adding the herbals and the white petals and spices. Pour in the milk and honey, and then enter the tub through the gateway you have created. The mixture has a sweet-smelling aroma. Enjoy this and allow it to inspire positive images in your mind. Dunk yourself in this water five times. As you emerge from each dip, feel yourself opening up to the positive energy in the world around you, as a petal opens up to the rising of the sun.

When you are finished, step out of the tub. With an empty cup, once again scoop out the contents of the bathwater. If you used whole nutmegs, try to have at least one in the cup. Drain the rest of the water. Allow yourself to air dry and then step outside. This time, you will be facing the East. Instead of holding the water above your head, hold it close to your chest and say these words:

"I welcome this day with joy and gladness. I open myself to the blessings that the world has to offer me. I attract light, love, and positivity to every area of my life. I welcome all the good spirits into my heart and my home."

Toss the water in the direction of the rising sun. You feel like immediately washing off all that egg gunk in your hair but resist the urge. Give yourself time to absorb all the positive energy that the ritual has provided by waiting until you are completely dry.

Conclusion

Voodoo is one of many contemporary folk religions in Africa which emerged from traditional African spirituality. Voodooism encompasses the observance of rites, rituals, and ceremonies which form part of a traditional belief system. The tradition is widely practiced in Haiti and the Dominican Republic, where slaves work plantations from West Africa. It is also practiced in New Orleans and elsewhere in the southern United States, particularly since the African diaspora brought many enslaved West Africans to New Orleans (Hoodoo).

Voodoo rituals are also practiced in many parts of the West Indies. Voodoo as a religion or practice has been frequently stereotyped in popular and fringe literature, with depictions ranging from the ridiculous to the grotesque. It also exists in forms that show voodoo as a practice that is used for individual empowerment and physical healing, with practitioners drawing on African spiritual traditions and Catholic symbolism to create unique syncretic faiths.

Ceremonies in voodoo practice are usually conducted during a working session, lasting several hours. In this period, the practitioner may use their knowledge of herbal remedies, medical herbs, or spells to heal other people and cause harm to others. They may also make use of ritual tools, such as the voodoo doll. In the practice of sorcery, various methods are used to control the soul and gain access to powers that are believed to be exerted by other entities. These entities can be seen as spirits or gods who influence a certain domain. Thus they become the source of power for activities in connection with this sphere.

For many people, the Voodoo religion is a mystery, full of secrets and spells, rituals, beliefs, traditions, and rites that others may misunderstand. It is not a world authority or a holy book. It places a greater emphasis on community and encourages each person's unique experience, responsibility, and empowerment.

As a result, it's not uncommon to hear and see a lot of misconceptions about it, as well as bad portrayals. Fortunately, you have been allowed to change that through this book, which tries to educate you on the true nature of Voodoo. I hope it has given you a better understanding of Voodoo and how it encompasses and encompasses every facet of human experience. As a result, it is unquestionably one of the most important and valuable faiths ever created.

Made in United States
North Haven, CT
25 October 2023

43154810R00070